While the Kettle Boiled:

The Power of Now

**Small moments. Big shifts.
Five minutes at a time.**

DAVINA VIDLER

Copyright © 2025 by Davina Vidler

All rights reserved, including the right to reproduce this book or portions thereof in any form whatsoever.

Publisher:
Australian Self Publishing Group, Pty. Ltd. / Inspiring Publishers
PO Box 159, Calwell, ACT 2905, Australia.
Phone: 61-(0) 2 6291-2904
http://australianselfpublishinggroup.com

A catalogue record for this book is available from the National Library of Australia

National Library of Australia Prepublication Data Service

Author: Davina Vidler

Title: **WHILE THE KETTLE BOILED: The Power of Now**

Sub-Title: **Small moments. Big shifts. Five minutes at a time.**

Genre: Non-Fiction - Self Help

ISBN: 978-1-923449-55-8 (PBK)

Dedication:

For everyone who thought they didn't have time.

To Ken,
who has spent a lifetime whispering, *"slow down"*
while I raced to keep up with the world.
You've been my still point in the storm,
my quiet encouragement,
my biggest believer.
You remind me every day that presence is power —
and love, when lived fully, is enough.

And to my children,
who keep teaching me how to grow,
how to soften,
how to rise.
You are my reason, my rhythm, and my becoming.

Preface

This book was born in my kitchen. Not in a writing retreat or a quiet study, but in the soft hum of everyday life — between medications and meals, between care and chaos, while the kettle boiled and the cat curled on the windowsill and my husband, Ken, rested in his bed. It came to me one day, not as a flash of brilliance, but as a whisper. I was standing by the kettle — exhausted, overwhelmed, waiting for five minutes of hot water — and I thought, "What if this is it? What if this is the time I've been waiting for?"

So, I wrote one sentence.
And the next day, I wrote another.
I didn't wait until I felt ready.
I didn't clear my schedule or fix my life.

I simply showed up, tired but willing, for five minutes at a time. We are so often waiting for "someday." For the house to be quieter, the children to be older, the work to be lighter. For more energy, more inspiration, more permission. But life doesn't pause. And your dreams? They're still there — whispering, waiting, hoping you'll listen. *While the Kettle Boiled-The Power of Now* is a gentle invitation to start now. Not in spite of your busy life, but within it. Not when you feel strong, but because you feel called. This book is for everyone who has ever said, "I wish I had more time." It's a reminder that even the smallest pockets of stillness — five quiet minutes, a cup of tea, a window of breath — are enough to come home to yourself.

Whether you use this book to write, to notice, to rest, or to dream again, I hope it becomes a small act of reclaiming.

A tiny revolution in a chipped mug.

A return to wonder.

A beginning.

Meet the Author

My name is Davina Vidler. I'm a nurse, a mother of nine, a grandmother of eight, a postgraduate student, and a full-time carer for my husband, Ken, who lives with advanced secondary progressive multiple sclerosis.

Our days are shaped by routines that don't pause. Medications, repositioning, emotional care, advocacy. Homeschool lessons, uni assignments, work, mothering, caring. Love, exhaustion, and fierce tenderness all share the same space. I wrote this book not from a place of ease, but from a place of feeling overwhelmed — and hope. There was a time when I felt like I had nothing left for myself. I had dreams — to write, to grow, to rediscover the parts of me that weren't only caregiver or nurse — but no time, no energy, and no space.

And then one day, while the kettle boiled, I paused.
Just for five minutes.
And I began.

That's where this book came from — five minutes at a time. As a nurse with a background in holistic care, I've long believed in tending to the whole person — body, mind, and spirit. But in my own life, I had forgotten to tend to myself. *While the Kettle Boiled-The Power of Now* became my way back.

While the Kettle Boiled: The Power of Now

This book is for the people like me who feel like their life doesn't leave room for creativity, rest, reflection, or healing. For those who are too tired to start big, but brave enough to begin small.

I believe the world is moving too fast. We're rushing past the sacred, the ordinary, the chance to hear our own souls speak.

I want the world to slow down — not in grand, sweeping changes, but one person at a time.

One breath.
One cup of tea.
One moment of noticing.

One of my favourite scripture says, "Be still, and know that I am God." For me, that is not a physical stillness, it's a stillness of heart and mind, and stillness begins with slowing down.

But I also know that some of us — carers, parents, frontline workers — can't always slow down. I can't.

So instead, we grab the moments we can. The five minutes while the kettle boils.

And we start there.

You don't need more time, more money, or more perfection.

You just need the moment you already have.

Let this be that moment.

— Davina

Contents

Before You Begin: A Gentle Invitation................ 11

The Practice 12

   Chapter 1 The Steam Is Rising...................................... 13

   Chapter 2 The Lie We Live ("I'm Too Busy").................. 15

   Chapter 3 The Courage to Create 17

   Chapter 4 The Blank Page Smiles Back........................ 19

   Chapter 5 What I Could Do Instead 21

   Chapter 6 The Comparison Trap 23

   Chapter 7 Tiny Joys... 25

   Chapter 8 My George McFly Moment........................ 27

   Chapter 9 A Window of Wonder 30

   Chapter 10 Reclaiming Quiet 32

   Chapter 11 A Cup of Stillness...................................... 34

   Chapter 12 Ritual, Not Routine 36

   Chapter 13 Five Minutes of Grace 38

   Chapter 14 Tired But Willing 40

Chapter 15 The Forgotten Self 42

Chapter 16 The Shadow That Follows 44

Chapter 17 Love Letter to the Woman at the Sink 47

Chapter 18 You Are Not Behind 50

Chapter 19 Nothing is Wasted 52

Chapter 20 One note at a Time 54

Chapter 21 Five Minutes, One Life 56

Chapter 22 Becoming Again 58

Chapter 23 When Strength Becomes a Wall 60

Chapter 24 Permission to Be... 63

Chapter 25 For Ken — The Quiet Strength 65

Your Personal Emotional Tool Kit 67

Personal Note 82

After the Steam Settles 84

Author Bio 86

Before You Begin:
A Gentle Invitation

Dear Reader,

Before you dive into these pages, I want to offer you something —

not instruction, not pressure... just invitation.

This is not a book you have to read cover to cover.

You may open it to any page. Read it with a warm cup in hand. Let it sit beside your sink, on your nightstand, in your bag.

This book isn't asking anything of you — only that you let its words meet you as you are.

Skip around. Scribble in the margins.
Read one line a day. Or binge it like your favourite show.

You don't need hours. Just moments. Kettle moments.

Because even in the time it takes to boil water, you are allowed to feel, reflect, breathe, be.

This is your space now. Welcome.

The Practice

These chapters are five-minute reflections, each paired with a quote, a journaling prompt, and space to write. Small moments of presence that create deep inner shifts.

A journey of a thousand miles begins with a single step.
Lao Tzu

Chapter 1
The Steam Is Rising

While the Kettle Boiled, I Started Anyway

Ken had fallen asleep. The morning had already been long — meds, breakfast, laundry, an emotional moment that left the room heavy. The air still held that weight, thick enough to taste.

I shuffled into the kitchen, my slippers dragging across the tiles. The kettle sat there like an old friend, waiting. Sunlight caught the lip of the sink, painting a thin gold line along the bench. I reached for the kettle, filled it, and realised I had five quiet minutes.

I almost opened Facebook. Almost answered emails. Almost convinced myself I was too tired to do anything else. My hand hovered over the phone — my autopilot escape route — but instead, my gaze fell on my laptop.

It was already open. A faint layer of dust sat on the corner of the keyboard, like it had been waiting for me. I clicked the file: Book Draft. The cursor blinked, steady and patient, as though it had been holding its breath for me to return.

So I wrote a sentence.

While the Kettle Boiled: The Power of Now

Just one. That's all I could manage. But the moment my fingers touched the keys, something shifted. The noise in my head dimmed. My breath slowed. It felt like lighting a candle in the dark — small, fragile, but warm enough to remind me I was still here.

Sometimes, the biggest shift doesn't feel like a thunderclap. It feels like steam rising — quiet, soft, but unstoppable.

 Quote:

> "Start where you are. Use what you have.
> Do what you can."
>
> — Arthur Ashe

 Reflection Prompt:

What's one thing you almost did instead of something that would bring you joy?

What could you try tomorrow, just during kettle time?

▬ Journaling Space:

While the kettle boiled today, I…

_____

_____

_____

_____

_____

(Write freely. A sentence is enough.)

Chapter 2
The Lie We Live ("I'm Too Busy")

While the Kettle Boiled, I Questioned "Too Busy"

"I'm too busy."

I've said it so many times it could be my signature. I've said it to my children, to my friends, to myself. I've whispered it like an apology and declared it like a badge of honour.

One Tuesday morning, I caught myself mid-sentence. The dishwasher was humming, Ken's medication schedule sat on the bench, and my phone screen was lit with half-finished messages. I told a friend I couldn't call her back because I was "too busy"… but then I stood there scrolling through an online shop I didn't even need.

Busy had become my alibi — the perfect shield for the things I was avoiding. If I was "busy," I didn't have to risk starting the thing I longed for but feared failing at. I didn't have to make space for myself in a life already too full.

While the Kettle Boiled: The Power of Now

But that day, while the kettle began its low growl, I looked up from my phone. I saw five unclaimed minutes. And I claimed them. I jotted down a chapter idea. I sent a quick voice memo to a friend I love.

I closed my eyes and dreamed.

I realised I wasn't too busy. I was just distracted. Scattered. Afraid to choose me.

Now, when I hear that old phrase creep back in, I try to rewrite it:

"I'm allowed to start small."

"I'm worthy of five minutes."

"I have time — when I choose to honour it."

 Quote:

> "You will never find time for anything.
> If you want time, you must make it."
> — Charles Buxton

 Reflection Prompt:

When was the last time you said, "I'm too busy"? What were you avoiding or protecting?

Where in your day might five quiet minutes be hiding — not to add pressure, but to reclaim peace?

▰ Journaling Space:

While the kettle boiled today, I challenged the idea that I'm too busy. I noticed…

_____

_____

_____

_____

_____

_____

_____

Chapter 3
The Courage to Create

While the Kettle Boiled, I Made Something That Was Mine

It's not that I didn't want to create — I just didn't think I was allowed to. Not with dishes in the sink. Not with Ken needing me. Not with assignments due and laundry waiting and a to-do list that never ends.

But deep down, I was craving it. A moment that was mine. Not to be productive — but to feel alive.

That morning, I grabbed a pen while the kettle hissed, and steam curled into the air like a ribbon of possibility. I doodled. I wrote a single poetic line. I rearranged some words in a file I hadn't opened in months. And for five minutes, I was not just a nurse, carer, mother, or student. I was an artist. A writer. A dreamer. It wasn't perfect. But it was mine.

Creative courage isn't loud. It doesn't need a studio, a sabbatical, or silence. It just needs a sliver of space. A willingness to begin. And a whisper of self-trust: This matters. I matter.

Quote:

"The desire to create is one of the deepest yearnings of the human soul."
— Dieter F. Uchtdorf

 Reflection Prompt:

What creative part of you have you silenced or buried under "real life"?

What would it mean to let her speak — just for five minutes?

Journaling Space:

While the kettle boiled today, I let myself create. I...

_____

_____

_____

_____

_____

_____

_____

_____

_____

(What came through you — a line, a sketch, a moment of colour or rhythm?)

Chapter 4
The Blank Page Smiles Back

While the Kettle Boiled, I Faced the Page

Some mornings, the page felt like a mirror I didn't want to look into. Too tired, too raw, too unsure of what I had left to say.

But I showed up anyway. I'd hover my fingers above the keyboard, frozen.

One rainy afternoon, the kitchen light was soft and gold. The kettle was starting its slow hum. I sat down anyway, my tea bag waiting in the cup beside me. The page stared back — not accusing, not impatient — just there. A small, open space.

I typed one line. Deleted it. Typed another. This one stayed. It wasn't profound. It wasn't polished. But it was true. And in that moment, I realised the blank page wasn't a threat — it was an invitation. An invitation to turn inward, to listen, to see what was ready to be said.

It didn't have to be perfect. It didn't even have to be good. It just had to be honest.

Sometimes, the best thing we can bring to the page is ourselves — messy, uncertain, but willing.

Five minutes. One page. A sigh of relief.

 Quote:

> *"Start writing, no matter what.*
> *The water does not flow until the faucet is turned on."*
> — Louis L'Amour

 Reflection Prompt:

What have you been afraid to face — on the page or in yourself?

What could you whisper to a blank page today?

Journaling Space:

While the kettle boiled today, I faced the page. I…

_____

_____

_____

_____

_____

_____

_____

_____

Chapter 5
What I Could Do Instead

While the Kettle Boiled, I Reached for Something Different

I almost scrolled. My hand was already halfway to my phone. It's a habit — unconscious, automatic, easy.

But that day, I paused. The kettle hadn't even started boiling yet. And I thought, what could I do instead?

I could stretch. I could write a line. I could breathe deeply. I could just stand in my own skin and not abandon myself for a screen.

There is nothing wrong with wanting escape — sometimes it's necessary. But not every impulse needs to be indulged. And not every spare moment needs to be filled.

Sometimes, reclaiming our attention — even for five minutes — is an act of profound resistance. An act of coming home.

 Quote:

"Almost everything we do is out of habit. The question is: is it a habit of survival or a habit of becoming?"
— Unknown

Reflection Prompt:

What do you usually do in your in-between moments?

What is one small shift you could make today — just for you?

Journaling Space:

While the kettle boiled today, instead of reaching for distraction, I...

_____

_____

_____

_____

_____

_____

_____

_____

_____

Chapter 6
The Comparison Trap

While the Kettle Boiled, I Remembered My Own Path

I saw someone on Instagram who wrote a whole book in three months. Someone else had a morning routine, six kids, and somehow perfect skin.

I looked at my broken nails, Ken's med paperwork on the table, the basket of laundry, and I almost closed the laptop again.

Comparison is the thief of everything: joy, time, momentum, peace.

But while the kettle boiled, I breathed. I remembered that person isn't me. They don't live my life, carry my weight, or dream my dreams.

So, I wrote my sentence. Planted my seeds. Took five minutes for my purpose.

Someone else's chapter isn't your timeline. Their page isn't your failure. Their life isn't your measurement.

This is your journey. Your voice. Your story. And it's still unfolding.

Quote:

"Don't compare your beginning to someone else's middle or your middle to someone else's end."

— Jon Acuff

 Reflection Prompt:

Who or what are you comparing yourself to right now?

What is one thing you can do your way, in your time?

Journaling Space:

While the kettle boiled today, I came back to my own path. I…

_____

_____

_____

_____

_____

_____

_____

_____

Chapter 7
Tiny Joys

While the Kettle Boiled, I Noticed the Good

The teacup was chipped, but the tea was warm. The cat stretched, her spine arching like a drawn bow before she settled into her favourite patch of sunlight. Outside, a bird landed on the fence and tilted its head, as if it had a secret just for me.

None of these moments changed the world. But they changed me.

I used to rush past them. My eyes were trained to hunt for what was urgent, broken, or unfinished: the unpaid bills on the counter, the laundry basket looming in the hallway, the emails that multiplied overnight. My focus was a spotlight fixed on what needed fixing.

One afternoon, though, I let the kettle time lead me somewhere else. I leaned against the counter and let my eyes wander. That's when I saw it: a magpie balancing on the top rail of the fence, its beak glinting in the light. It hopped twice, then tossed something shiny into the air and caught it again, like it was playing a private game.

I don't know why that tiny scene felt so important. Maybe because it was proof that life was happening in little bursts of joy, right here in the middle of my ordinary.

Tiny joys don't announce themselves. They wait quietly for you to notice. A first sip of coffee. A word that lands just right. A memory that makes you smile instead of cry.

When I started collecting them, one by one, I realised they were mending me. Small stitches in a heart that had been worn thin.

Joy doesn't have to be loud to be powerful. Tiny joys accumulate.

And if you let them, they'll stitch a weary heart back together, one gentle thread at a time.

 Quote:

"Enjoy the little things, for one day you may look back and realize they were the big things."
— Robert Brault

 Reflection Prompt:

What small thing brought you comfort today?

If you gave joy your attention — even for five minutes — what might you notice?

▬ Journaling Space:

While the Kettle Boiled: The Power of Now

While the kettle boiled today, I noticed...

Chapter 8
My George McFly Moment

While the Kettle Boiled, I Realised I Was Hiding

In the Bob Zemeckis, Stephen Speilberg 1985 film 'Back to The Future' (one of my favourite films) there's this quiet moment that always stops me. Marty discovers his dad, George McFly, writes science-fiction stories. When Marty asks to read them, George shrinks back.

"What if they didn't like them? I don't think I could take that kind of rejection."

The first time I heard it, I laughed. The tenth time, I felt the sting. By the twentieth, I realised George was holding up a mirror.

That was me.

I'd been doing it for years — writing in the margins of my life, keeping poems tucked away like secrets, carrying dreams too tender to name. Not because I didn't believe in them... But because I wasn't sure I could handle the ache of someone else not believing in them.

I thought if I stayed hidden, I'd be safe. But hiding came at a cost: Disconnection. Silence. Loneliness. My daughters saw my strength, but not my soul. They didn't know I was a writer. A dreamer. A woman with whole worlds inside her.

Then came the day I read a poem aloud to my daughters. My hands shook so much I had to steady the page against the bench. My throat felt tight. They listened — really listened — and when I finished, there was this pause. Not awkward. Sacred.

"You wrote that?" one of them asked, eyes wide.

"Yes," I said, my voice quieter than I meant it to be.

Something shifted in that pause. The air between us felt warmer, closer. They saw me — not just the mother, the carer, the strong one — but me.

Maybe you've had a George McFly moment too. Maybe there's a story inside you, a song, a painting, a part of your heart, that's never been seen.

I want to tell you: it's okay to be scared. But don't let fear be the author of your life.

Even five minutes of courage — while the kettle boils — can change everything.

 **Quote:**

> "A ship in harbor is safe —
> but that is not what ships are built for."
> — John Shedd

Reflection Prompt:

Is there something you've kept hidden because rejection feels too big to bear?

What would it feel like to let someone see it — even a little?

Journaling Space:

While the kettle boiled today, I thought about my own George McFly moment. I...

_____

_____

_____

_____

_____

_____

_____

_____

Chapter 9
A Window of Wonder

While the Kettle Boiled, I Looked Outside

I used to rush past the window. Too much to do. Too many things waiting. But then one day, while the kettle rumbled and the morning light shifted just so, I looked up.

And there it was: A sky like a watercolour painting. A magpie walking with purpose. The apple tree quietly blooming, even though no one had told it to.

Wonder is always waiting — but it will not shout. It arrives in whispers, in pauses, in glimpses. And often, it lives right outside your window.

These small acts of noticing are sacred. They remind us that beauty doesn't need to be earned. That the world keeps offering softness, even when life feels sharp.

We don't need to go somewhere special to be awed. We just need to look.

Quote:

*"Instructions for living a life: Pay attention.
Be astonished. Tell about it."*

— Mary Oliver

 Reflection Prompt:

What did you see today that made you pause — even for a second?

When was the last time you let yourself feel wonder?

▰ Journaling Space:

While the kettle boiled today, I noticed…

_____

_____

_____

_____

_____

_____

_____

_____

_____

Chapter 10
Reclaiming Quiet

While the Kettle Boiled, I Turned Down the Noise

The radio was on. Notifications pinged. Ken was resting, but my mind wasn't — it was scrolling, spinning, solving.

I almost didn't notice the kettle.

That's when I realised: I hadn't heard silence all day. Not true silence — not the kind that lets your thoughts settle, or your soul whisper something back.

So I turned it all off. And in the hum of the kitchen, with only the sound of water heating and my own breath, I felt something loosen inside me. Like a crowded room finally emptying out. Like coming home to myself.

We are constantly inundated — with news, noise, needs. But quiet isn't just a break. It's a return. To what matters. To what waits. To who we are when no one's watching.

You don't need to go away to find peace. You just need five minutes. A kettle. And the courage to turn the volume down.

Quote:

*"Silence is not the absence of something,
but the presence of everything."*
— Gordon Hempton

 Reflection Prompt:

Where in your day is there noise that could be replaced with stillness?

What does your inner voice say when you let it speak?

Journaling Space:

While the kettle boiled today, I reclaimed quiet. I noticed…

___

___

___

___

___

___

___

___

Chapter 11
A Cup of Stillness

While the Kettle Boiled, I Let It Be Enough

The world is loud. Even in my own home — even in my own body — there are days when the noise never stops. The beeping of machines. The ticking of clocks. My constant mind chatter. The long list of things left undone. The wrestle between what I want to do verses what I have to do.

But then there's the kettle. The slow, rising hum. The warmth in my hands. The gentle pause between one task and the next.

And if I listen closely enough, I can almost hear it: Be still, and know that I am God. Not in thunder. Not in fire. In stillness.

Stillness is not doing nothing. Stillness is doing one thing fully.

Sitting. Sipping. Noticing the steam. Letting my shoulders drop. Letting the moment be a container for grace.

Some mornings, all I can manage is a single sip in silence. But in that sip, I return to myself — and to something greater than myself. A cup of stillness becomes communion. A kettle becomes an altar.

And I remember: I don't need to perform to be held. I don't need to hurry to matter. I can be still. And that is enough.

 Quote:

> *"Be still, and know that I am God."*
>
> — Psalm 46:10

 Reflection Prompt:

What does stillness mean to you — beyond quiet?

When was the last time you truly paused — and how did it feel?

▄ Journaling Space:

While the kettle boiled today, I poured a cup of stillness. I noticed…

_____

_____

_____

_____

_____

_____

_____

_____

_____

Chapter 12
Ritual, Not Routine

While the Kettle Boiled, I Made it Sacred

At first, it was just a routine. Boil the kettle. Make the tea. Get on with the next thing.

But something shifted when I began showing up with intention. Lighting a candle. Taking a deep breath. Noticing how the steam curled in the air like a gentle prayer. Letting my mind slow down enough to see what was right in front of me.

That's when it became a ritual.

Routines get us through the day. Rituals remind us why we're moving through it in the first place.

You don't need incense or silence or ceremony. You just need presence. The quiet decision to mark a moment as meaningful — even if no one else sees it.

Now, when I make tea, I do it slowly. When I journal, I do it with reverence. When I take five minutes for myself, I let it be holy.

Because your life isn't made of grand milestones. It's made of small, sacred repetitions — turned toward joy.

 Quote:

"Rituals are the formulas by which harmony is restored."
— *Terry Tempest Williams*

 Reflection Prompt:

What parts of your day feel rushed or automatic?

How could you turn one into a ritual of care?

▪ Journaling Space:

While the kettle boiled today, I honoured this moment. I…

_____

_____

_____

_____

_____

_____

_____

_____

_____

Chapter 13
Five Minutes of Grace

While the Kettle Boiled, I Gave Myself Permission

Grace isn't just for other people. It's for the weary woman who snapped at her partner because she was too tired to cry. It's for the carer who forgot a dose, then blamed herself all day. It's for the artist who hasn't painted in months. It's for you. It's for me.

One Thursday morning, I was standing at the counter, eyes gritty from lack of sleep, hands resting on the edge of the bench. I hadn't ticked off half the things I'd planned. My body ached, my mind was foggy, and that old voice started up: You should be doing more.

Then the kettle began it's gentle hiss, I stood still — not to plan or write or clean — but to forgive myself.

For not being perfect. For not being everything to everyone. For trying — and sometimes failing.

I whispered aloud, "You're doing the best you can. And that is enough."

That one sentence softened everything.

Five minutes of grace can shift an entire day. Because grace is not a reward for getting everything right — It's the permission to love yourself when you don't.

 Quote:

> *"Grace means that all of your mistakes now serve a purpose instead of serving shame."*
> — Brené Brown

 Reflection Prompt:

What have you been hard on yourself for lately?

What would it feel like to forgive yourself — even a little — while the kettle boils?

Journaling Space:

While the kettle boiled today, I gave myself grace for…

_____

_____

_____

_____

_____

_____

_____

(Write it like you'd write to someone you love. Because you are someone you love.)

Chapter 14
Tired But Willing

While the Kettle Boiled, I Showed Up Anyway

I didn't have much left in the tank. My body was aching. My brain foggy. Ken had had a rough night, and I'd been in helper mode since sunrise. The to-do list still loomed like a shadow at the edge of my vision.

I stood at the kitchen bench, waiting for the kettle to boil, wondering if I had anything left to give myself.

But something stirred inside me — not energy, exactly... more like willingness. A soft, stubborn part of me that whispered, "Five minutes. Just five. Not for them. For you."

So I picked up a pen. I opened the notepad. I stretched my arms toward the sky. I didn't feel ready, inspired, or particularly alive — But I was willing. And that was enough.

There is a kind of power in tiredness — A quiet strength that says: I am weary, but not done.

We don't need to be full of fire to begin. Sometimes we light the match because we are cold.

Quote:

"Courage doesn't always roar. Sometimes it is the quiet voice at the end of the day saying, 'I will try again tomorrow'."
— Mary Anne Radmacher

 Reflection Prompt:

What would it look like to honour your tiredness and your willingness today?

What might you give yourself — even if it's just a breath?

Journaling Space:

While the kettle boiled today, I showed up — tired, but willing. I…

_____

_____

_____

_____

_____

_____

_____

_____

_____

Chapter 15
The Forgotten Self

While the Kettle Boiled, I Remembered Me

In the quiet moments, as the kettle hums and steam curls into the air, I catch a glimpse of someone I used to know—me. Not the caregiver, the student, or the parent, but the dreamer, the artist, the woman who found joy in simple things.

One afternoon, I was making tea when an old song came on the radio. Without thinking, I hummed along. In that moment, I was back in my twenties, dancing barefoot in the kitchen, hair loose, laughing with no idea what was coming next in life. I realised she's still here — that younger version of me. She's just buried under schedules and caregiving and the weight of so many roles.

Life's responsibilities often overshadow our essence, but these brief pauses offer a chance to reconnect. As the water warms, I breathe deeply, recalling the passions and dreams that once ignited my spirit.

Reconnecting with oneself doesn't require grand gestures. Sometimes, all it takes is a moment of stillness, a deep breath, and the willingness to remember.

 Quote:

*"Almost everything will work again
if you unplug it for a few minutes, including you."*
— Anne Lamott

 Reflection Prompt:

What aspects of yourself have you set aside in the busyness of life?

How can you honour and nurture those parts of you today?

Journaling Space:

While the kettle boiled today, I reconnected with…

_____

_____

_____

_____

_____

_____

_____

_____

_____

Chapter 16
The Shadow That Follows

The Shadow That Follows

There's a shadow that follows me. It doesn't shout, it whispers.

What if you're not enough? What if you're too much? What if they leave? What if it's all for nothing?

I didn't always know it was fear. Sometimes it wore different clothes — perfectionism, over-giving, silence, anger, withdrawal.

It showed up in my need to prove myself. To fix everything. To hold everyone together, even when I was breaking.

But while the kettle boiled one ordinary afternoon, I met my fear face to face.

It wasn't a monster. It was a younger version of me, still waiting to be chosen. Still waiting to be held.

I saw her — the girl who watched her parents leave. The girl who felt invisible unless she performed. The woman who kept giving until there was nothing left.

I placed the kettle down. And I whispered something she'd never heard before.

You are safe now. You don't have to earn love. You don't have to disappear to be accepted. You are allowed to take up space.

Fear still visits sometimes. But now I invite it in for tea. I no longer run.

I sit beside it and say, I see you. I hear you. But you don't get to drive today.

 Quote:

> "I learned that courage was not the absence of fear, but the triumph over it."
>
> — Nelson Mandela

 Reflection Prompt:

What fear has followed you silently — not the loud kind, but the quiet one that shaped your choices?

When did it first appear?

What did it teach you — and what would it mean to walk forward without it leading?

While the Kettle Boiled: The Power of Now

▬ Journaling Space:

While the kettle boiled today, I wrote............This page is for your shadow — not to banish it, but to understand it.

Let it speak. Let it soften. Let it sit beside you without driving.

_____
_____
_____
_____
_____
_____
_____
_____
_____

You are safe here. No one has to see this but you.

Chapter 17
Love Letter to the Woman at the Sink

While the Kettle Boiled, I Remembered Her

Dear one,

I see you.

I see the way you keep going — quietly, constantly — in a world that rarely pauses to notice. I see the dishes you wash, the medications you give, the meals you make, the tears you blink away so no one sees.

You hold up the world with tired arms and a soft heart. And I know there are days you wonder if anyone sees the weight you carry — or how gently you carry it.

This is your reminder: You matter. Not because of what you do, but because of who you are. A woman who keeps choosing love, even when no one is watching.

You are not just doing chores. You are holding space. You are not just scraping plates. You are feeding souls. You are

While the Kettle Boiled: The Power of Now

not just cleaning up. You are creating room for rest, for care, for breath.

And even if no one says thank you — I will.

Thank you for showing up. Thank you for staying when it would be easier to run. Thank you for choosing tenderness in a world that forgets to be soft.

May your kettle time become sacred. May your reflection look back with pride. May you remember: the woman at the sink is not invisible. She is a warrior. A healer. A lighthouse.

She is you.

With love, Davina

 Quote:

> "The world is changed by your example,
> not by your opinion."
> — Paulo Coelho

 Reflection Prompt:

When was the last time you thanked yourself?

What would a love letter from you to you sound like today?

▪ Journaling Space:

While the kettle boiled today, I offered myself love. I wrote…

Chapter 18
You Are Not Behind

While the Kettle Boiled, I Let Go of the Clock

There's a lie that haunts us — especially women, carers, creatives, and dreamers: "You're behind."

I've heard it whisper in lecture halls when I was older than most of my classmates. I've heard it in waiting rooms, watching younger women chase careers while I juggled caring for Ken. I've felt it scrolling through social media — seeing houses bought, trips taken, goals ticked off.

But one day, while the kettle hissed and my to-do list stared back at me like a disappointed teacher, I realised: behind what, exactly? Who drew this map I'm trying to follow? And why am I holding myself hostage to it?

Time is not a race. Healing is not a timeline. Dreams do not expire.

Your path is not broken because it looks different. You are not late. You are becoming.

I remembered the year I started university at forty-one, surrounded by students young enough to be my children.

I thought I was late to the party. But it turned out the party was better because of the path I'd walked to get there.

That day, I put the list down, breathed in the rising steam, and whispered, "I'm not behind. I'm right here."

And right here was enough.

You're not too old. It's not too late. And your pace — whatever it is — is sacred.

 Quote:

> *"No one is ahead of you. No one is behind you.*
> *You are exactly where you need to be."*
> *— Steve Maraboli*

 Reflection Prompt:

Where in your life do you feel "behind"? Whose story are you comparing yourself to?

What might it feel like to believe you are right on time?

▬ Journaling Space:

While the kettle boiled today, I released the rush. I reminded myself…

_____

_____

_____

_____

_____

Chapter 19
Nothing is Wasted

While the Kettle Boiled, I Reframed the Past

There are parts of my story I used to hide. False starts. Delayed dreams. Chapters full of pain or doubt or just… survival.

But as I stood by the kettle that day — weary, wiser — I realised: Nothing was wasted.

Not the heartbreak. Not the missed chances. Not even the days that felt like they slipped through my fingers.

Everything I've lived has shaped this moment. The strength I have now? It was forged in those quiet, unseen places. The compassion I offer others? Born from the nights I wept alone.

Even my delays taught me timing. Even my detours taught me depth.

You don't have to be proud of every page. But you can honour them all. Because every part of your story has brought you here — And here is holy ground.

Quote:

"Out of suffering have emerged the strongest souls; the most massive characters are seared with scars."
— Kahlil Gibran

 Reflection Prompt:

What part of your story feels wasted or unfinished?

What gift might it secretly hold?

🖊 Journaling Space:

While the kettle boiled today, I honoured my story. I remembered…

_____

_____

_____

_____

_____

_____

_____

_____

Chapter 20
One note at a Time

While the Kettle Boiled, I Learned Something New

I always wanted to play the piano.

Not professionally. Just... beautifully. To sit down, let my fingers speak, and let the music say what words couldn't.

But for years, I told myself it wasn't the right time. Too busy. Too tired. Too old. Too expensive. And learning music was something you did as a child. The idea of beginning in my fifties was ridiculous.

Then one day, I sat in on my youngest daughter's piano lesson. I watched her learn. One key at a time. And I realised — maybe it's not too late. Maybe I don't need hours to begin. Just a few quiet minutes.

So I bought a piano-for-beginners book. And during kettle time — between caregiving and coursework and everything else — I practiced. Slowly. Imperfectly. And now? I can read music. Not fluently. Not fast. But enough. Enough to make a sound that feels like mine.

Stillness doesn't always mean silence. Sometimes it sounds like progress — one note at a time.

 Quote:

> "You don't have to be great to start.
> But you have to start to be great."
>
> — Zig Ziglar

 Reflection Prompt:

What have you always wanted to try but never gave yourself permission to begin?

What would five minutes of practice look like today?

Journaling Space:

While the kettle boiled today, I took a step toward something I've always wanted. I...

_____

_____

_____

_____

_____

_____

_____

_____

Chapter 21
Five Minutes, One Life

While the Kettle Boiled, I Chose to Begin

Five minutes doesn't seem like much. But five minutes of courage? Five minutes of truth-telling? Five minutes of showing up for yourself?

It can shift everything.

One day you write a sentence. The next, a paragraph. One day you breathe deeply. The next, you remember who you are.

It's not about productivity. It's about presence. And presence adds up. Five minutes becomes a rhythm. A rhythm becomes a return. A return becomes a life you're proud to live — from the inside out.

We don't need to escape to transform. We just need to come home to the moment we already have.

Five minutes. One kettle. One life.

Quote:

*"Great things are not done by impulse,
but by a series of small things brought together."*
— Vincent Van Gogh

 Reflection Prompt:

What could five minutes today contribute to your one precious life?

What truth are you ready to return to?

▬ Journaling Space:

While the kettle boiled today, I chose presence. I…

_____
_____
_____
_____
_____
_____
_____
_____
_____

Chapter 22
Becoming Again

While the Kettle Boiled, I Grew a New Beginning

Becoming isn't something we do once. It's something we do over and over again — quietly, bravely, imperfectly.

Some days I feel like I'm starting from scratch. Other days, I remember how far I've already come. But every time I pause — truly pause — I feel something inside me rooting deeper.

The world says we need to reinvent. I say: we need to return.

Return to wonder. Return to joy. Return to who we were before we forgot ourselves.

Five minutes isn't a finish line. It's a doorway. And every time you walk through it, you become again.

 Quote:

> "And the day came when the risk to remain tight in a bud was more painful than the risk it took to blossom."
>
> — Anaïs Nin

Reflection Prompt:

What part of yourself are you ready to meet again?

What would it feel like to begin — gently — today?

Journaling Space:

While the kettle boiled today, I returned to myself. I...

Chapter 23
When Strength Becomes a Wall

While the Kettle Boiled, I Let Them See Me

There was a time when I thought strength meant holding everything together. For my children. For my husband. For the world.

I didn't cry much. I didn't crumble. I just did what needed to be done. And they all saw me — capable, organised, unwavering. But they didn't feel me.

And somewhere along the way, that strength built walls. Walls that kept them safe — but also kept me out. My daughters saw my effort, but not my softness. They felt my support, but not my love.

I didn't know how to be vulnerable. It terrified me.

But then, something changed. I started writing again. Poetry at first — small, trembling lines that carried things I couldn't say aloud.

And one day, I shared one with them.

My hand shook. My heart pounded. But I let them read it. And in that moment, something cracked open — in me, and between us.

It didn't fix everything. But it was real. And real is where reconnection begins.

Creative courage isn't just about making art. It's about making space. For our truths. For our softness. For our healing.

Even if it's just for five minutes. Even if it starts with a single line. Even if your voice shakes.

The blank page is sometimes safer than a spoken word. But once we fill it, it can become a bridge. And that bridge can save something sacred. It hasn't knocked all the walls down, but it's made doors in them. And sometimes, when I'm brave enough, I open one.

 Quote:

> *"Vulnerability is not winning or losing;*
> *it's having the courage to show up*
> *when you can't control the outcome."*
> — Brené Brown

 Reflection Prompt:

What part of you have you hidden behind strength?

What might be waiting on the other side of one small act of creative courage?

While the Kettle Boiled: The Power of Now

▬ Journaling Space:

While the kettle boiled today, I let myself be seen. I…

_____

_____

_____

_____

_____

_____

_____

_____

Chapter 24
Permission to Be...

**While the kettle boiled,
I gave myself permission.**

To be...

- tired, without apology
- quiet, without guilt
- joyful, without a reason
- selfish, when I needed space
- messy, undone, and still beloved
- not okay, and not explain why
- alone, without being lonely
- brave in small ways
- still learning
- held, even when I didn't ask to be
- imperfect, but present
- angry, but soft-hearted
- unsure, but still stepping forward
- enough. Just enough. Always enough.

Some days that meant letting the dishes wait. Some days it meant being joyful for no reason. Some days it meant not having to explain why I was quiet, or why I didn't want to answer the phone.

Giving ourselves permission isn't indulgence. It's honesty. It's recognising that being human means needing rest, space, joy, stillness, and sometimes even solitude.

As the kettle hissed, I wrote them down: tired without apology, quiet without guilt, brave in small ways, enough — always enough.

The water clicked off. I poured the tea. And I felt lighter.

You have permission, too

Permission to pause. To breathe. To be human.

While the kettle boils — let it be your invitation to release every 'should' and just be.

 Quote:

"Give yourself permission to be where you are, to feel what you feel, and to let go of the need to be anything else."
— Morgan Harper Nichols

 Reflection Prompt:

Finish this sentence: "If I truly believed I was enough, I would give myself permission to…"

What part of yourself have you been silencing or shrinking to meet others' expectations — and what might shift if you gave that part permission to speak?

▰ Journaling Space:

While the kettle boiled today, I gave myself permission. I…

Chapter 25
For Ken – The Quiet Strength

**While the kettle boiled,
I thought of you.**

Of all the mornings when the pain etched deeper lines into your face, but you still managed to smile.

Of how you listen more than you speak, and when you do speak, every word matters.

You have taught me more about strength than any book, more about grace than any church, more about love than any fairy tale ever dared to promise.

You are my still point in a turning world.

Even now — especially now — you anchor me. Not because you fight your battles loudly, but because you face them quietly. With dignity. With faith. With that half-smile that tells me, we're okay.

You are not just part of my story. You are the still breath between the lines.

Quote:

"Strength does not come from physical capacity. It comes from an indomitable will."

— Mahatma Gandhi

 Reflection Prompt:

Who is your still point in a turning world — and how do they show up for you, again and again?

How can you honour them today?

Journaling Space:

While the kettle boiled today, I cherished those who anchor me by…

_____

_____

_____

_____

_____

_____

_____

_____

_____

Your Personal Emotional Tool Kit

Read This When...

A gentle library of reminders for the moments you forget your strength.

These pages are not chapters to be read in order — they're lifelines.

Choose the one that whispers to you in the moment.

Let it hold you for five minutes.

☕ **Read this when you're overwhelmed...**

   Stop.
   Place your hand on your heart.
   Take one breath — just one.
   You are allowed to pause.
   You are allowed to feel it all.
   This is not the end of you.
   It's just a hard moment.
   Even now, the kettle is boiling.
   The world is making space for you to begin again.
   What is making you feel overwhelmed? Noise? Endless to-do list? etc

📝 Prompt:

- When did you last feel seen and supported?
- What is one gentle thing you can do for yourself today?

☕ Read this when you feel invisible...

You are not a ghost.

I see you.

You are doing sacred work, even if no one applauds.

Even if no one comes.

You are not failing — you are *faithful*.

And that is enough.

📝 Prompt:

- What would it look like to show up for yourself today?
- Who makes you feel visible and valued?

☕ Read this when you think you should be stronger by now...

Strength isn't the wall.

It's the breath you take when the wall rises up again.

It's the softness you protect.

Let yourself be tired. Let yourself be real.

Strong doesn't mean invincible. It means *still here*.

Even superwoman needs a break

It is okay to ask for help.

🖋 Prompt:

- What does real strength look like in your life?
- When were you quietly strong and no one knew?

☕ Read this when you think it's too late…

It isn't.

You are not too old, too slow, too behind.

The dream didn't expire.

It just waited.

Begin now.

Begin again.

Five minutes is enough.

🖋 Prompt:

- What is one thing you've done later in life that made you proud?
- If there were no clock, what would you begin today?

☕ Read this when you miss the person you used to be…

She's not gone.

She's just under the noise.

Look for her in small joys.

A quiet cup of tea.

A laugh that surprises you.

A song you forgot you loved.

She's still there — becoming something new.

📝 Prompt:

- What do you miss about the person you used to be?
- What do you love about the person you are now?

☕ Read this when you're grieving...

Grief has no manners.

It doesn't knock.

It doesn't wait until you're ready.

Some days it's a whisper. Some days it's a wave.

Let it come. Let it speak.

You don't have to be brave right now.

You just have to breathe.

Your love didn't die.

It lives in memory, in ritual, in every tender ache.

📝 Prompt:

- Who or what are you grieving?
- How can you honour them in the present moment?

☕ Read this when you can't get out of bed...

Your body is tired because your soul is carrying a lot.

Rest is not failure.

Stillness is not surrender.

You are allowed to lie still.

Even flowers bloom from dark soil, unseen.

If you do one thing today, go sit out in the sun

While the Kettle Boiled: The Power of Now

📝 Prompt:

- What is your body trying to tell you right now?
- What would feel comforting — even if it's small?

☕ Read this when you don't like who you see in the mirror...

Be gentle.

She's been through more than most will ever know.

She has carried children, grief, meals, and secrets.

She has stayed when others left.

You don't have to love her today.

But you can stop judging her.

Start by placing your hand on her cheek — and whispering, *thank you*.

📝 Prompt:

- What is one thing you're proud of in yourself — not for how you look, but for how you love?
- Can you thank your body for something today?

☕ Read this when you're caring for someone else and feel like you're disappearing...

You are not invisible.

You are the quiet heartbeat in the background.

The unsung note in the harmony.

The reason someone else gets another chance.

And you matter too.

Even caregivers need care. Even you.

🖋 Prompt:

- What do you need to feel like *you* again?
- What part of yourself is still waiting to be seen?

☕ Read this when everything feels like too much...

Put one hand on your chest.

Say it with me: "Just this breath. Just this moment."

You don't have to solve everything today.

You don't have to be everything today.

You just have to come back to now.

One kettle-minute at a time.

🖋 Prompt:

- What is one thing you can let go of right now?
- What helps you return to now?

☕ Read this when you feel alone...

You may not hear the echo yet, but your voice still matters. Somewhere, someone is breathing easier because of something you did.

You are not forgotten. You are not a mistake.

You are a thread in someone else's becoming.

Even now, you are being held.

🖋 Prompt:

- Who makes you feel safe — even in memory?
- What would you say to someone else feeling this way?

☕ Read this when you're afraid of the future...

You don't have to know what comes next.

You only have to be here.

The next breath.

The next sip.

The next note of the song.

Let tomorrow worry about itself.

You're not walking into the unknown alone.

You're bringing every brave moment that led you here.

📝 Prompt:

- What truth do you know for sure, right now?
- Can you name one thing you've survived that proves your strength?

☕ Read this when someone you love won't speak to you...

I know the ache. The silence that thunders.

You replay every word, every moment.

You wonder what could've changed it.

But you are not only the mistakes.

You are also the love that tried.

The forgiveness you offer in secret.

You are still worthy of connection.

Still worthy of peace.

📝 Prompt:

- What would you say if you had the chance — without fear?
- What part of your love still speaks, even in silence?

☕ Read this when you feel burnt out...

Exhaustion is not weakness.

It's a signal.

It means your body and heart need time to mend.

You were never meant to be a machine.

Even fire needs tending.

Even you.

Step back.

Soften.

Nothing falls apart when you rest.

Sometimes, that's when things fall *into place*.

📝 Prompt:

- What is one thing you can say no to today?
- What brings you rest — not just sleep, but restoration?

☕ Read this when you wonder if your work matters...

It does.

Even if it's unfinished. Even if it's unseen.

Even if it's just a sentence scribbled while the kettle boiled.

You are making something out of nothing.

You are creating light.

That's holy work.

📝 Prompt:

- What has someone thanked you for — even once?
- Where do you see your quiet impact?

☕ Read this when you're doubting your purpose...

Purpose doesn't always roar.

Sometimes it whispers in the way you make someone feel seen.

In the cup of tea you bring.

In the story you keep telling.

You don't have to change the world.

Just touch one heart.

That is enough.

📝 Prompt:

- What lights you up — even for a moment?
- When did you last feel like your presence made a difference?

☕ Read this when you feel like you're starting over — again...

You're not back at the beginning.

You're beginning from experience, from wisdom, from strength you didn't have before.

This is not failure. This is evolution.

And it's brave every single time.

📝 Prompt:

- What have you learned from the last time you began again?
- What part of you is stronger now?

☕ Read this when you think no one understands...

Maybe they don't.

But I promise you this — someone has stood barefoot in pain and kept walking.

Someone else knows the sound of their own silence.

And someone is reading this right now, whispering, *me too*.

📝 Prompt:

- What would you want someone to know about your story?
- When did you last feel understood — even by yourself?

☕ Read this when you're scared to rest...

Rest is not lazy. It's holy.

It's the space between what was and what will be.

Even the ocean needs a tide. Even your breath needs a pause.

You were never meant to run without stopping.

📝 Prompt:

- What does rest mean to you — beyond sleep?
- What might soften if you allowed yourself to stop?

☕ Read this when you need to forgive yourself...

You did the best you could with what you knew at the time.

And now you know more. Now you see differently.

That's growth — not guilt.

Forgive the woman you were. Honour the woman you're becoming.

Both have carried you here.

📝 Prompt:

- What do you wish someone else would forgive you for?
- Can you say to yourself: I did the best I could?

☕ Read this when you feel like giving up...

Don't.

Not tonight.

You've come too far to stop here.

You don't need to climb the mountain.

Just take one more breath.

One more moment.

Hope doesn't always shout — sometimes it just waits quietly until you're ready.

So far you have survived 100% of your worst days.

📝 Prompt:

- What has kept you going before — even once?
- What might hope look like in just one breath?

☕ Read this when you feel too much...

Your sensitivity is not a flaw.

It's your superpower.

You feel deeply because you love deeply.

You notice what others miss.

The world needs your tenderness.

Don't harden — soften wisely.

📝 Prompt:

- What have your feelings helped you understand more deeply?
- Where has your sensitivity been a strength?

☕ Read this when you can't stop crying...

Let the tears come.

They are evidence of your humanity, not your weakness.

You are not broken.

You are washing grief with truth.

Crying is remembering you still feel — and still care.

📝 Prompt:

- What are the tears trying to say?
- What would it feel like to let them fall without shame?

☕ Read this when you're not sure who you are anymore...

Identity can unravel in caregiving, in crisis, in loss.

But that doesn't mean it's gone.

You are still you — changing, growing, hidden beneath the layers of survival.

Let yourself be found again. One tiny joy at a time.

✍ Prompt:

- What words feel true about who you are right now?
- What part of you do you want to rediscover?

☕ Read this when you feel joy and guilt at the same time...

It's okay to smile even while healing.

It's okay to laugh while grieving.

You don't have to earn joy.

Let it visit you like sunlight — even through a window of sorrow.

✍ Prompt:

- When did joy surprise you recently?
- Can both grief and joy hold hands in this moment?

☕ Read this when you're waiting for permission...

This is it.

This is your permission slip to rest, to write, to create, to care for you.

No one else gets to tell you when it's your turn.
Let this be your beginning.

📝 Prompt:

- What would you do today if no one could say no?
- Can you offer yourself the yes you're waiting for?

☕ Read this when you feel numb...

Sometimes the heart protects itself by going quiet.
Numbness is not failure — it's a survival rhythm.
Stay close.
Stay gentle.
The feeling will return.
And when it does, you'll still be here — ready to feel it all.

📝 Prompt:

- What used to bring you comfort when things felt flat?
- What tiny spark could you follow right now?

☕ Read this when you're afraid to hope...

Hope has hurt you before.
But please don't confuse disappointment with destiny.
Hope isn't a promise — it's a posture.
You can stand in it quietly, without needing proof.
Just open the door a crack. Hope will find the rest.

While the Kettle Boiled: The Power of Now

🐾 Prompt:

- What does hope look like in the smallest form today?
- What would it feel like to leave the door cracked open?

☕ Read this when you wonder if you're making a difference...

You are.

In ways you can't always measure.

In moments that feel too small to matter.

The kindness you offered, the listening, the presence — it ripples.

You may not see it, but you are a light.

🐾 Prompt:

- Who would miss you if you stopped showing up?
- What act of kindness did you offer that you didn't think anyone noticed?

Personal Note

There are parts of my story that don't always make it to the page. But they live beneath every word I write.

I didn't grow up with stillness. I grew up with suitcases, silence, and survival. By eight, I was the one making sure my little world didn't fall apart. By fifteen, I was homeless. Working four jobs. Still trying to finish school. The world expected me to carry on — so I did.

I've worn many names since then: daughter, mother, caregiver, nurse, student, advocate, wife. Some were given. Some I earned. There's a kind of grief that doesn't announce itself — it just settles into your bones and teaches you how to keep breathing.

My husband was diagnosed with MS at 38. Our grandson — a light we all loved — was lost in a tragedy too big for language. And now, my daughter, her mother-heart shattered, no longer speaks to me.

This book wasn't written in some serene retreat. It was written between loads of laundry, hospital visits, and whispered tears. It was written in stolen minutes — while the kettle boiled. And somehow, those minutes saved me.

I don't offer answers. I offer presence. Not perfection, but practice — of noticing, of breathing, of being in the now. Of reclaiming moments that seemed too small to matter. But they mattered. They always did.

This book is a love letter — To the woman at the sink. To the caregiver, the quiet creator, the woman who keeps showing up. To you.

You're not behind. You're just in the middle of becoming. And right now — right here — is holy ground.

After the Steam Settles

The kettle boiled. The words came. Some days gently, like steam unfurling at dawn. Other days, they arrived heavy, with the weight of everything I hadn't yet said aloud.

This book was never about perfection. It was about presence. It was about reclaiming five quiet minutes in a world that doesn't pause for anything — except maybe a kettle.

You've read my reflections. Maybe you've seen yourself between the lines. The mother. The dreamer. The carer. The one who stayed. The one who still whispers, there must be more than this — even while folding laundry or holding grief in one hand and a spoon in the other.

If you've reached this page, know this: You didn't just read. You held space — for yourself, and for me. You walked beside me, note by note, page by page, moment by moment.

So now I invite you — To keep writing. To keep noticing. To keep becoming. Even when it's messy. Especially then.

Because presence is not a destination. It's a practice. A sacred rebellion against the rush.

And you — You are not behind. You are just in the middle of remembering who you were, and who you are becoming next.

With all my love,
Davina

Author Bio

Davina Vidler is a nurse, mother of nine, grandmother of eight, postgraduate student, and full-time carer for her husband, Ken, who lives with advanced progressive MS. Drawing from a life steeped in caregiving, grief, and quiet strength, Davina writes with gentle clarity and fierce tenderness. Her work honours the everyday moments where presence becomes power, and small rituals offer deep healing. *While the Kettle Boiled* is her first book — a love letter to women who give their all and are learning to return to themselves, five minutes at a time.